Torchlight

PETER MCDONALD was born in Belfast in 1962, and was educated at Methodist College, Belfast, and University College, Oxford. After winning the Newdigate Prize and an Eric Gregory Award, he published his first book of poems in 1989. Two further collections have been published by Carcanet Press. His critical and editorial work includes *Mistaken Identities: Poetry and Northern Ireland* (1997), *Serious Poetry: Form and Authority from Yeats to Hill* (2002), and *The Collected Poems of Louis MacNeice* (2007). He has taught at the Universities of Cambridge and Bristol and, since 1999, he has been Christopher Tower Student and Tutor in Poetry in the English Language at Christ Church, Oxford.

Also by Peter McDonald from Carcanet Press

Pastorals
The House of Clay

PETER McDONALD

Torchlight

CARCANET

Acknowledgements

Grateful acknowledgement is made to the editors of the following publications, in which some of these poems first appeared: *Archipelago*, the *Edinburgh Review*, the *Guardian*, *Oxford Poetry*, *PN Review*, *Poetry Review*, the *Scottish Review of Books* and the *Times Literary Supplement*. Some poems were also published in *Love Poet, Carpenter: Michael Longley at Seventy* ed. Robin Robertson (Enitharmon Press, 2009), and *Joining Music with Reason: 34 Poets, British and American, Oxford 2004-2009* ed. Christopher Ricks (Waywiser Press, 2010).

First published in Great Britain in 2011 by

Carcanet Press Limited
Alliance House
Cross Street
Manchester M2 7AQ

A CIP catalogue record for this book is available from the British Library

ISBN 978 1 84777 091 2

The publisher acknowledges financial assistance from Arts Council England

Supported by
ARTS COUNCIL
ENGLAND

Typeset by XL Publishing Services, Tiverton
Printed and bound in England by SRP Ltd, Exeter

Contents

I

II

III

I

The Neighbours

In the single-bedroom flat I used to cry the night through
as my mother walked the floor with me, rocked me and fed me
past the small, insensible hours, not to wake the neighbours;
though often upstairs there might be half the Group Theatre
going till daybreak – a tiny, bohemian airpocket:
Jimmy Ellis (in the Group, before *Z Cars*), or Mary O'Malley,
and over from next door, next door but one maybe, George
McCann, Mercy Hunter, John Boyd and the BBC,
talking politics or shop, intrigue or gossip the night through.

But perhaps on this occasion there's only the baby
cutting in and out of silence in a high spare room
where the McCanns have just lodged their visiting poet
who by noon will cross from the Elbow Room to the studios
in Ormeau Avenue, and deliver his talk, unscripted,
on 'Childhood Memories'; whose sleep now, if sleep it is,
remains unbroken through the small, insensible hours
between the whiskey nightcap and a breakfast of whiskey.

The Weather

Weightless to me, the heavy leaves
on a sumach drag down their long stems
ready to fall, and spend their lives
on one inflamed, extravagant
display, when light like the rain teems
over and through them; ruined, pendant,
parading every colour of fire
on a cold day at the edge of winter.

They are like the generations of man
of course, and we knew that; we knew
everything pretty much in advance
about this weather, light like the rain,
the red-gold and the gold tattoo
that dying things can print on ruin
(no ruin, in fact, except their own),
flaring up even as they go down.

The sunshine makes reds virulent
and yellows vibrant with decay;
it's not surprise, more like assent
when they fall, when I let them fall,
to what is fated, in its way,
of which this rain-cleared light makes little,
meaning the day can gleam, can glow:
and not a bad day, as days go.

Singles

Unprotected for the most part, out of their paper sleeves,
and stacked in the sideboard as if it were a jukebox
with all of their nicks and scratches and sharp scores
pressed up together in the plastic-smelling dark,

the singles used to spill out like so many side-plates
once I got started on their daily inspection;
tilting the vinyl into sunlight, and closing one eye,
I squinted across the surface, over a dark

spectrum of grooves and dust, where the smooth run-out
ended at a milled ridge, then the label
in blue or black, with its silver-grey lettering
that I learned by heart, spelling the titles and names

slowly to myself, more certainly each time,
to put together words like Gloria, Anna-Marie,
and whole runs of language in THE HUCKLE-BUCK,
SHE LOVES YOU, or SORRY (I RAN ALL THE WAY),

as I ferried singles across our quiet sitting-room
to the Dansette with its open lid, a spindle
and rubber-plated turntable, ready to play them all
to destruction, till late in the morning, when

the patterned carpet was the map of another world
in some year that's not coming around again,
like the showbands and Them, the Beatles and Jim Reeves,
and THIS BOY, DISTANT DRUMS, or BABY PLEASE DON'T GO.

Reversing Around a Corner

Plato could have handled it: the turns,
half-turns and quarter-turns, the speed
and timing are abstract concerns
to be perfected in your head
before they enter the world of sense
and take you on a perfect course
back and around, intelligence
working with gentleness or force
on your hands and feet, your busy eyes
in that manoeuvre – the very one
I fluffed (to nobody's surprise)
in my first test, and now, umpteen
years later, somehow I get right
exactly, without thinking, here
between your house and a building-site
across the road, in reverse gear
and barely glancing back, at best,
as I point myself the other way
(on what, you tell me, is a test-
route) easily, with enough play
in the wheel to give the look of ease
now it can hardly matter, now
there's no one but myself to please,
and rules, and what the rules allow,
don't figure, now there are times when
nothing is beautiful, or true,
with no great difference between
what I can do and I can't do.

Rainbow Ribbons
1980

At the mid-point of a working day
we are the solitary couple
in the Botanic's upstairs lounge,
I with my sweet Martini, sweetened
with lemonade, where feathers of ice
make little prisms in the glass,
she with the same, as indoor lights
on the thousand and one tight black
curls and ringlets of her hair
create their own fair weather,
tumbling and falling like ribbons.

When we step into a sun-shower,
I press her close to kiss
wet hair that is springy and firm
and turns to a whole dark spectrum
as fast clouds hit and miss
each other over our heads, giving
a light so clear it never goes
back exactly as it was.

The Reeds

On my own now with the lake, lake-water's
suck and slap against a wooden jetty
accompanies the solitary, middle-distance
heron that my eyes follow in its take-off
and heavy flight beyond their farthest reach.

★

I can walk for yards across these narrow planks
and touch the tips of reeds on either side
of me, where they come level with my arms:
the reeds move in the water as they give
under my hands, then come back to their places.

★

To see her arms and long wrists in the water,
her fingers slim and definite as reeds,
would be too much, and in the building quiet
admit that now, when nobody can hear,
it might be a relief to scream aloud.

★

As I turn towards the interrupted noise
where reeds are parting for me like a sea,
my heron circles back from the far shore,
aloof, but still checking on everything
in the water, to see what is really there.

Green Tea

That morning, when I was half-way
to all the way lost, the clouds
seemed to make way
for more clouds in a busy sky;
the path I wanted was one towards
the town, was it? This was country,
and the more progress I made,
it was more, and not less, countryside.

As I confess how I lust after
fluency, and how I distrust it,
fluent with light
our green tea fills the fragile cups
(I am too early or too late,
retracing, is it, my own steps),
cups that are luminous
with a whole language unknown to us.

A day when nothing really gets done,
when sentences break up, and when
nothing avails
against the clinches, snares and toils
of words that want not to be plain,
is it, or not to be held down,
not held to what I mean:
I mean a day much like this one,

between half-way to utter waste
and all the way, when bits of the past
count as pure loss
against the tea leaves' secret signs,
visible, not readable – unless
to my grandmother and her dead friends
where they sit beyond recall,
cups in hand, in the parlour still.

Boiled, but not boiling, water stains
slowly where now it gives back the
glow of the sun
in a cup that's made of porcelain,
and the leaves settle down exactly
across each other, one on one,
each more than half the way
to all the way askew, awry.

A Pair of Shoes

Pencil strokes shine like pewter or gunmetal
over the flimsy paper where you drew
these empty sneakers for no reason at all,
and I look through
them to your words on the other side
that say so little, I can't decide
how to construe

the precise lines and the shadows you worked out
across those crumply shoes, as if they fell
down together, in freakish window-light
starting to fail
on a day full of rain, when the whole sky
comes down with just itself to see by,
so you can't tell

colours apart from versions of grey and white
in the instant that you're taken by surprise —
a silver flash, wings maybe, with eyesight
not the right size
to see whatever's flying; almost
enough, when in daylight the ghost
opens its eyes.

Oxford Poetry

i.m. M.I.

1

You weren't there, but your typescript had arrived
an hour before the copy went to press:
one of us took a bus up the Cowley Road
to get the piece of paper to the printers,
a sheet where every other line was stiff
with Tippex, and over the patches your own hand,
elegant even there, even in biro.
The finished magazines would be wheeled down
in a shopping trolley all the way to Magdalen,
and where they went from there I never knew,
preoccupied with typos I might find,
too late to fix, in something on my watch.
I was the careless one, and still am careless,
for whom your nickname, which was maybe half-
affectionate, of 'Supermac' was apt,
satirically two decades out of date
(I'd told you about how I sent the real
Harold Macmillan gently off to sleep
by spouting verse in the Sheldonian).

I missed things, often. It wasn't until
one afternoon with you, deep in the Chequers,
at a sunny table, drinking like we meant it,
when we were joined by an ancient, fugitive
Glaswegian who talked rubbish for an hour,
and my accent softened, and your open smile
broadened and shone, accepting, that I knew
my stupid blunder in taking you for English.
We weren't in Oxford, even though we sat
in High Street – not *that* Oxford, anyway,
where power hatches and speaks to itself:
we were at home in feeling far from home,
and listening to a voice that wasn't ours,

while in the sunlight I could see you make
connections and corrections both at once.
The blunders of a quarter century
all felt like nothing once I stood apart,
a year ago today, watching them wheel
you out from Magdalen, when you weren't there.

2
13 March, 1972

A typist has got it wrong, and so in pen
the Foreign Secretary corrects his memo,
adding the phrase she left out from his last
sentence of para. 1, in which 'Our own
parliamentary history is one long story
of trouble' is missing three vital words:
he dashes in *with the Irish*, and now it's clear.

The rest is all right: he tells the PM
how they (the Northern Irish) 'are not like
the Scots or Welsh', he tells him how he doubts
they ever will be, how the British interest
is not served best by 'tying them closer
to the United Kingdom'; he recommends
pushing them now towards a United Ireland.

He is himself a Scot: Eton and Oxford
(3rd Class in Modern History), a life
given largely to service, and being spent so now,
adding the weight of his practised signature
as he sends the paper on to Downing Street
like a coda to one long story of trouble
from Alec Douglas-Home (a Christ Church man).

3

Trip-switches tripping, rooms and rooms of them;
all the connections failing one by one;
power and poetry riddled with each other:
the information, accurate and mad,
of a spent lifetime, what does it come to?
One kind of answer is a bare report,
its commentary an open smile – yours;
then a thousand lightbulbs switching themselves off.

The Interruption

Somebody almost takes the call
just when a phone stops, their slow
story reaching the point, maybe,
while three or four others vacantly
wait for the spirit to move: but now
a story with nobody in it
barges straight in, in a flash,
before they can make themselves heard
or finish, before they can start.

Nobody says another word
as all of them hear the silence start;
they just take stock as if, oh,
they see now, and their faces fall.

August, 1998

Draught

He runs cold water into a glass
where he stands in the Braniel kitchen
at the sink, just home from work,

and raises that glass to his stubbled lips
and drinks, and drinks it down in one;
a good draught, he says, of Adam's ale.

★

The kitchen where I can reach the tap
with a long tumbler that came free
from the Maxol station at Gilnahirk

and top up the glass with barley water
then balance it back to head-height,
pausing before the first big gulp.

★

No more than once a week, he takes
the car down to McGowan's for
ten shillings' worth of petrol, waits

as the lad at the pumps goes to fetch
free cutlery (a knife, a spoon)
or glassware; Green Shield stamps.

★

Light from the backyard brings to life
that pale grey liquid in my glass,
and shows how little things have settled;

I watch the turns and twists, like dust-
motes, of all the sunned-on barley-
flecks suspended in the water.

★

When I swallow, sometimes there's a long
moment when all the drink is cold
in my chest, when it's a cold hand

laid on my breastbone, and the odd
time when the water fills me up
past any thirst that it can quench.

Canopic Jars

1
Lights

When they had done their job
of making good the air
I breathed, with a last sob
these lungs, that couldn't bear
my weight, gave up on me;
they had emptied themselves out
of speech and secrecy,
of confidence and doubt;
now they could give no more:
silence was really death,
surface really the core;
the soul was really breath.

2
Liver

Hidden again from view,
this organ is at rest
from the thing it had to do
unheeded, unaddressed,
a lifetime long; no more
to work with blood and bile,
here it is deep in store
like an unconsulted file
padded with lost routine,
long past the moment now
when perhaps there might have been
some use for it, somehow.

3
Intestines

Rewound here, and closed in,
these yards of underground
cabling can begin
to turn themselves around
one last time, and as if
they knew what they had done
digesting all that life
slowly, but by the ton,
they must, they can, give up:
just to support a man
who took, from plate and cup,
from jug, oven, or pan
all he could touch or taste,
they made from what he tried
and the small lives that died
in tens of thousands, waste.

4
[Heart]

This jar contains my heart:
when it had beaten its last,
they placed it here apart
from me, or from what passed
for me, as a special case –
unlike Egyptians, who
would keep the heart in place
beneath linen and glue
inside a corpse's chest
to be a quickened seed
as the body rose again,
convinced these were the best
pains to have taken when,
really, there was no need.

Slowest

for Andrew McNeillie

When the first rockets tore
in at an angle
they left behind nothing
but concrete and steel,

flowers, and weeds flowering
over the bitter soil.
After four years, my
first flowers of jasmine

take me by surprise,
five-petalled, weightless,
and all but forgotten
in this dust-heavy garden,

yet their perfume identical
to what I remember
in the marble and worked stones
slowly persisting

close to the sea,
where jasmine curled up
with weeds and wild roses
one evening in Tyre.

Portrush

I don't know if they ever met in life,
but today the spirits of two dead poets
keep us company as we dash through rain
all the way from the West Strand into town;
Jimmy is about forty, his wild hair
fighting the elements; Archie is wearing
an enormous pullover made for the north,
conspicuous still as the only black man
about here: it rains so hard that our scalps
and our backs ache with it, as Jimmy dodges
quickly into the Northern Counties Hotel
(which isn't here any more) to have a last one,
and Archie heads for that Chinese restaurant
where he brought me once a lifetime ago.
But I'm not able to perform introductions
– Archie I met the once, Jimmy I hadn't
seen for a dozen years before he died
(I owed him better, and neglected him) –
and you and I are shocked by the brutal downpour
plastering us when we've only stopped for chips,
for which, now we're here, we don't have the heart.

Later

But for the time, I would tell you
about a garden in Gilnahirk
(above the road, where you drive through
every morning to get to work),
a garden not there any more
around the red-brick council cottage
kept up by Ruby and James Moore,
where flowers flowered over the edge
of a steep path, over the walls
and into each other's beds; where lines
of bright, new-planted annuals
criss-crossed and trespassed from their lanes
all summer; where the roses flared
and flaunted along trellises, and where
a row of vegetables was cleared
of weeds each morning; a place for sheer
toil in a builder's few spare hours,
working the ground for food and show,
the gable wall a wall of flowers,
the glen in darkness far below:
and I would tell you everything
about that garden, now the land
has been churned up and cleared, to bring
a chip shop and a second-hand
tyre depot, now that it's all gone,
now James and Ruby are in their grave
at Comber, tell you every one
of the flowers I used to pick and save
from flowerbeds filled up to the brim
and over it, but for the time.

II

Augury

A sound from above like ripped material,
but the bright level clouds are nearly too bright
for me to see what's moving there, the small
dagger-stabs and arrows of birds in flight,
hurling themselves, and pausing, and shooting by:
a dozen swifts unravelling the sky.

A Castaway

When he was washed up naked on the shore
Odysseus improvised a suit of leaves
and clothed himself in that: with nothing more
to lose, with nothing to conceal from thieves,

in one sense, if no other, he was free:
the ground was moving still with the waves' sway;
all his belongings were across the sea
and unimaginably far away;

his body, in the glare of early sun,
was solid, battered, with scars everywhere,
and his face, where so much salt water had run,
was creased to the touch, fragile in the air;

his arms, that lately held a woman close
and hooped her waist, and pressed her to the bed,
the hands that touched her where and how he chose,
that stroked her breasts, and felt her lips, now bled

where splintered wood and rocks in a great storm
had torn them; right down to his shoulders hung
the straggly hair, brittle with salt; his form
in its sand-shadow was bent, no longer young,

for he could not see himself as she had seen him,
although she knew he was a mortal man,
and he searched for fresh water that would clean him,
washing the sea from him, and the leathery tan,

but nothing now could rinse away the years
that clung to him, or those pains his body kept
close as its welts and bruises, close as hairs
on his strong chest, where Penelope had slept.

The Difference

Resourceful as he was, he seemed destined
to be always at the mercy of some
fate or other, his wily spirit twinned
with a targeted body, lashed and battered numb

by the sea, or whatever made the sea move
against him resolutely, tirelessly,
and put him always at one further remove
from the far island where his home might be;

now wet sand with its lines of twigs and stones
like fragments of an indecipherable text,
feathers and shells, seaweed and cast-off bones
wherever one wave stood in for the next

said nothing on this earth is a substitute
for anything else (warm light, a dab of rain,
the tide advancing backwards foot by foot,
flowers in the dunes not coming back again),

so he stared at the face of a faceless ocean
which never would hold still or clarify,
dark to look at, but flashing back the sun
like wine pouring itself out endlessly,

alone with all his plans and his misfortunes
distinct in the light and untranslatable,
knowing himself to be what he thought once
absurd, a man whose cunning and sharp will

were useless, and for all his intelligence
a prisoner in his own life, with no key
or no lock to turn: it was the difference
between the sea and his words for the sea.

The Harbour

Later, he thought about all the disguises
that worked for long enough to do the job,
the dirt and a tattered coat just compromises
with how things might be, once the seasons rob

someone of all their human shape and height,
no matter how upright they were or brave,
tear them with hunger, sap them of all fight,
and set them destitute beside the grave;

those roles of his, and all the assumed names,
details of lives that he could still recall
but never lived, life-stories that made games
from people who were never him at all

seemed less important now, now he was back
at some point after the whole story ended,
only himself again, on that worn track
between town and the harbour, with clothes mended

like his bones, searching the skyline all day
but seeing only sunlight over the waves,
odd shapes on water coming or going away,
never those shore-spirits from sandy caves

or girls standing beside freshwater springs
in conversation, watching him from afar
– nymphs, as it turned out – never those things
that had made his story from mischance and war

larger than any life he could design
out of his own experience and wit,
and never the goddess: the goddess who, when
you see her face, you can't imagine it.

Penalty

The clouds are blue with electricity and rain.
I have bared my head, and walk in a clammy afternoon
with purpose, quickly, skin and clothes stuck with sweat,
like someone searching for treasure, or for a lost child,
desperate under this watchful, unanswering sky;
leaves turning here all point in a single direction
as something touches faintly the hairs on my arms and legs:
it lifts hairs on my shoulders, hairs on my chest,
but without laying hands on me, my unclean flesh
slickened and used and tired, and sore and very old,
that watches out now for a first glance of lightning,
not knowing when or from where it will come, but knowing
that wisdom is to expect death, and fear the goddess.
The clouds are blue with electricity and rain.

Hymn

Greek, sixth century BC

This is about Demeter, the long-haired goddess
Demeter, and about her child, a skinny-legged
little girl who was just taken away
one morning by Hades, Death himself, on the say-so
of his brother Zeus, the deep- and wide-bellowing God.

She was apart from her mother, and from Demeter's
protecting sword, made all of gold, when he came;
she was running about in an uncut spring meadow
with her friends, the daughters of the god Ocean,
and picking flowers here and there – crocuses and wild roses,
with violets and tiny irises, then hyacinths
and one narcissus planted there by Gaia, the Earth,
as Zeus demanded, and as a favour to Death,
to trap the girl, whose own eyes were as small and bright
as the buds of flowers: it blazed and shone out
with astonishing colours, a prodigy as much for
the immortal gods as for people who die.
A hundred flower-heads sprung from the root
with a sweet smell so heavy and overpowering
that the wide sky and the earth, even the salt waves
of the sea lit up, as though they were all smiling.
The girl was dazzled; she reached out with both hands
to gather up the brilliant thing; but then the earth
opened, the earth's surface with its level roads
buckled, there on the plain of Nysa, and up from below
rushed at her, driving his horses, the king of the dead.

He snatched her up, struggling, and he drove her away
in his golden chariot as she wailed and shrieked
and called out loud to her father to help her,
to Zeus, the highest of high powers;
yet nobody – not one god, not one human being,
not even the laden olive-trees – paid heed to her;
but from deep in a cave, the young night-goddess

Hecate, Perses' daughter, in her white linen veil,
could hear the child's cries; and so could the god Helios
– god of the Sun, like his father Hyperion –
hear the girl screaming for help to Zeus, her own father:
Zeus, who was keeping his distance, apart from the gods,
busy in a temple, taking stock there of the fine
offerings and the prayers of mortal men.

For all her struggling, it was with the connivance of Zeus
that this prince of the teeming dark, the god with many titles,
her own uncle, with his team of unstoppable horses
took away the little girl: she, as long as she kept in sight
the earth and the starry night sky, the sun's day-beams
and the seas pulled by tides and swimming in fish,
still hoped, hoped even now to see her mother again
and get back to her family of the eternal gods.

From the mountain tops to the bottom of the sea, her voice
echoed, a goddess's voice; and, when her mother heard
those cries, pain suddenly jabbed at her heart: she tore
in two the veil that covered her perfumed hair,
threw a dark shawl across her shoulders, and shot
out like a bird across dry land and water,
frantic to search; but nobody – neither god, nor human –
was ready to tell her what had happened, not even
a solitary bird would give Demeter the news.
For nine whole days, with a blazing torch in each hand,
the goddess roamed the earth, not touching, in her grief,
either the gods' food or their drink, ambrosia or nectar,
and not stopping even to splash her skin with water.

On the tenth day, at the first blink of dawn, Hecate
came to help her, carrying torches of her own,
and gave her first what news she could: 'Royal Demeter,
bringer of seasons, and all the gifts the seasons bring,
what god in heaven, or what man on this earth
can have snatched away Persephone, and broken your heart?
I heard the sound of her crying, but I couldn't see
who it was; I'm telling you everything I know.'
Hecate said this, and received not one word in reply:

instead, Demeter rushed her away, and the pair of them
soon reached Helios, the watcher of gods and men.

Demeter stopped by his horses, and spoke to him from there.
'If ever I have pleased you, Helios, or if ever
I have done you a favour, do this one for me now:
my daughter's voice was lost on the trackless air,
shrill with distress; I heard, but looked and saw nothing.
You gaze down all day from the broad sky,
and see everything on dry land and the ocean:
so if you have seen who forced away my child
from me, and who went off with her, whether
a man or a god, please, quickly, just tell me.'
She said this, and the son of Hyperion replied:
'Holy Demeter, daughter of Rhea with her long hair,
you are going to hear it all – for I think highly
of you and, yes, I pity you, grieving as you are
for the loss of your skinny-legged little girl. So:
of all the immortal gods, none other is responsible
than the master of the clouds, Zeus himself, who gave her
to Hades his brother to call his own
as a beautiful wife. Hades with his team of horses
snatched her, and dragged her to the thickening dark
as she cried and cried. But come now; you are a goddess:
call an end to this huge sorrow; be reasonable:
there is no need for such uncontrollable rage.
Hades, the lord of millions, is hardly, after all,
the worst son-in-law amongst the immortals,
and he is your own flesh and blood, your own brother.
As for his position – well, he has what was allotted
originally, when things were split three ways,
the master of those amongst whom he dwells.'

So saying, Helios took up the reins, and his horses
were away all at once, bearing up the chariot
like birds with slender wings. And now grief fastened
– a harsher, a more dreadful pain – at Demeter's heart.
Furious with the black cloud-god, the son of Cronos,
she abandoned the gods' city, and high Olympus,
to travel through rich fields and the towns of men,

changing her face, wiping all its beauty away,
so that nobody, neither man nor woman, when
they saw her could recognise her for a goddess.
She wandered a long time, until she came to the home
at Eleusis of the good man Celeus, master there.

Heartsore, heart-sorry, Demeter stopped by the roadside
at the well they called the Maiden's Well, where people
from the town would come for water; sat in the shade
cast over her by heavy branches of olive,
and looked for all the world like a very old lady,
one long past childbearing or the gifts of love,
just like a nurse who might care for the children
of royalty, or a housekeeper in their busy house.
The daughters of Celeus caught sight of her as they came
that way to draw water, and carry it back
to their father's place in great big pitchers of bronze:
Callidice and Clisidice, beautiful Demo
and Callithoe, the eldest girl of all four,
more like goddesses in the first flower of youth.
They had no idea who she was – it's hard for people
to recognise gods – so they came straight up to her
and demanded, 'Madam, where have you come from
and who, of all the old women here, are you?
Why is it that you've walked out past the town
and don't go to its houses? Plenty of ladies
the same age as you, and others who are younger,
are there now, in buildings sheltered from the heat,
to welcome you with a kind word and a kind turn.'

When they had done, the royal goddess replied:
'Good day to you, girls, whoever you may be;
I'll tell you what you want to know, for it's surely
not wrong, when you're asked, to explain the truth.
I am called Grace – my mother gave me that name –
and I have travelled on the broad back of the sea
all the way from Crete – not wanting to, but forced
to make the journey by men who had snatched me,
gangsters, all of them. In that fast ship of theirs
they put in at Thoricos, where the women

disembarked together, and they themselves began
making their supper down by the stern cables.
But I had no appetite for any meal that they made,
and when their backs were turned I disappeared
into dark country, and escaped from those men
before they could sell me, stolen goods, at a
good price, bullies and fixers that they were.
That's how I arrived like a vagrant, and I
don't know what country it is, or who lives here.
May the gods who have their homes on Olympus
send you good husbands and plenty of children
to please the parents; but now, spare a thought
for me, like the well brought-up girls that you are,
and maybe I can come to one of your houses
to do some honest work for the ladies and gentlemen
living there, the kind of thing a woman of my age
does best: I can nurse a new baby, and hold
him safe in my arms; I can keep the place clean;
I can make up the master's bed in a corner
of the great bedchamber, and give all the right
instructions to serving women in the house.'

It was the goddess who said this; immediately
the girl Callidice, loveliest of Celeus' daughters,
spoke back to her, calling her Grandma, and saying:
'Whatever the gods give, however grievous the hardship,
people put up with it, as they must, for the gods
are that much stronger: it's just how things are.
But something I can do is tell you the names
of men who have power and prestige in this town,
who keep its walls in good shape, whose decisions
count for much, and whose advice is listened to here:
wise Triptolemus and Diocles, that good man
Eumolpus, then Polyxeinus, and Dolichus,
and our own dear father of course, all have
wives kept busy with the care of their houses;
not one of them would take a dislike to you
and turn you away from the door – they would welcome
you in, for there *is* something special about you.
Stay here, if you will, and we'll all run back

to tell our mother, Metaneira, the whole story,
then see whether she'll suggest that you come
to ours, and not go looking for another home.
She has a new baby in the house now, a son
born later in life, hoped for and prayed for:
if you were to take care of him, and see him through
to manhood, you would be the envy of any
woman, so well would that childcare be paid.'

Demeter simply nodded her head, and the girls
filled their shiny pitchers up with fresh water
and carried them away, their heads held high.
Soon they were at the family home, where they told
their mother all they had seen, all they had heard.
She ordered them to hurry back, and request this woman
to come and work for a good wage. So then
like deer, or like young calves in springtime,
happy and well-fed, running around in the fields,
they pulled up the folds of their long dresses
and dashed down the cart-track: the long hair,
yellow as saffron, streamed back over their shoulders.
They found Demeter where they had left her, by the road,
and they led her then towards their father's house
while she walked a little way behind, troubled at heart,
her head veiled, and with the dark dress fluttering
this way and that over her slender legs.

They got back to Celeus' house, and went in
through the hallway, where their mother was waiting,
seated by a pillar that held up the strong roof,
with her child, the new son and heir, at her breast.
The girls ran straight to her: slowly Demeter placed
a foot over the threshold, her head touched the rafters,
and around her the entire doorway lit up.
Astonishment and draining fear together shook
Metaneira; she gave up her couch to the visitor
and invited her to sit. But Demeter, who brings
the seasons round, and brings gifts with the seasons,
had no wish to relax on that royal couch, and she
maintained her silence, with eyes fixed on the floor,

until Iambe came up, mindful of her duty,
and offered a low stool, which she had covered
with a sheep's white fleece. The goddess
sat down now, and with one hand she drew
the veil across her face; and there she remained,
sunk in her quiet grief, giving to no one
so much as a word or a sign, sitting on there
without a smile, accepting neither food nor drink
for an age, as she pined for her beautiful daughter,
until Iambe, resourceful as ever, took
her mind off things with jokes and funny stories,
making her smile first, then laugh, and feel better,
and Metaneira offered her the cup she had filled
with wine, sweet as honey: but she shook her head
and announced that, for her, it was not proper now
to take wine – instead, she asked Metaneira
to give her some barley-water and pennyroyal
mixed up together: the queen made this, and served it
to the great goddess, to Demeter,
who accepted it solemnly, and drank it down.
Only then did Metaneira begin to speak:
'Madam, you are welcome here; all the more so
for coming from no ordinary stock
but, I'd say, from the best – for your every glance
is full of modesty and grace, you have something
almost royal about you. But what the gods give us,
hard though it is, we mere human beings
endure: all our necks are under that yoke.
You are here now, and whatever is mine shall be yours.
This little boy – my last born, scarcely hoped for,
granted me by the gods only after much prayer –
nurse him for me now, and if you raise him
to be a healthy, strong man, then any woman
at all will be jealous to see you, so great
will be the reward I give you for your work.'
Demeter replied: 'Accept my greetings, good lady,
and may the gods be kind to you. I will indeed
take care of this fine boy of yours, as you ask.
I shall rear him, and neglect nothing: sudden sickness
will never harm him, and never will some witch

of the forest, who taps roots for magic or poison,
touch a single hair of his head; for I know
stronger sources to tap, and I know the remedy
for all such assaults: a sure one, unfailing.'

Then with her two arms, the arms of a goddess,
she drew the baby in close to her own bosom,
and its mother smiled at the sight. In the big house
from then on Demeter looked after the son
of Celeus and Metaneira, while he grew up
at a god's rate, not eating solids, or taking
milk, but fed by her with ambrosia, as if
he were indeed a god, born of a god;
she breathed gently over him and kept him close,
and at night, unknown to anyone, she smuggled him
into the burning fire, like a new log of wood.
He was thriving so well, and looking so much more
than a human child, that both the parents were amazed.

And the goddess Demeter would have delivered him
from age and from death, had not Metaneira
been up one night and, without so much as
giving it a thought, from her own bedroom
looked into the hall: in sheer terror for the child
she screamed, and did her best to raise the alarm,
seeing the worst and believing it; she called out
to her little boy, half-keening: 'Demophoön,
my own baby, this stranger is hiding you
in the big fire, she's the one making my voice shrill
with pain, Demophoön, my darling, my child.'

She cried all this out, and the goddess heard her.
Furious that instant, mighty Demeter
took the child – their last born, scarcely hoped for –
and with her own immortal hands she brought him
out of the fire, set him gently on the floor,
then, brimming with anger, turned on Metaneira:
'You stupid creatures, you witless and ignorant
humans, blind to the good as well as the bad
things in store for you, and no use to each other:
I swear to you here, as gods do, by the rippling

dark waters of Styx, that I would have made
this child of yours immortal, honoured, a man
untouched by age for eternity; but nothing now
can keep the years back, or keep death from him.
There is one mark of honour that will always be his:
because he once slept in my arms, and lay in my lap,
all the young men at Eleusis, at the set time
each year, as their scared duty, will gather
for the sham fight, and stage that battle forever.
For I am Demeter, proud of my own honours
as the bringer of joy to the gods, and of blessings
to mortal men. Everyone now has to build me
a spacious temple, with its altar underneath,
by the steep walls of your city, where a hill
rises just above the Maidens' Well. The rites
will be as I instruct, when I teach you the ways
to calm my anger, and be good servants to me.'

And with that, instantly the goddess changed form –
her height, her whole appearance – shuffling away
old age, so that sheer beauty blazed and spread
in and around her; from her robes a gorgeous perfume
drifted, and from her immortal flesh there came
pure light, with the reach of moonbeams; her hair
flashed over her shoulders, and the entire house
was flooded with a sudden brilliance of lightning
as she stepped out through the hall. Metaneira's
knees went from beneath her, and for an age
she sat there speechless, not even thinking
to pick that dear child of hers up from the floor.

When his sisters heard the boy starting to cry
they jumped straight out of their beds, and one
caught him up in her arms, and held him close,
while another stoked the fire, and a third
dashed on bare feet to take hold of her mother
and help her away. As the girls huddled round him,
trying to comfort him and dab his skin clean,
the baby wriggled and fretted, knowing full well
these nurses were hardly the kind he was used to.

That whole night long, shaking with fear, the women
did their best to appease the great goddess.
When dawn came at last, they told everything
to Celeus, exactly as Demeter had instructed,
and he, as their ruler, lost no time
in calling the citizens together, and giving them
the order to build this goddess her temple
and to put her altar just where the hill rises.
They listened to him, and they did all that he said,
so that a temple rose up, as the goddess required.
When the job was done, and the people stopped working,
they all went home; but golden Demeter
installed herself in her temple, apart from the other gods,
and stayed there, eaten up with grief for her daughter.

She made that year the worst for people living
on the good earth, the worst and the hardest: not one
little seed could poke its head up from the soil,
for Demeter had smothered them all; the oxen
broke their ploughs and twisted them, scraping
across hardened furrows; and all the white barley
that year was sown in vain. She would have destroyed
every single human being in the world
with this famine, just to spite the gods on Olympus,
had not Zeus decided to intervene: first
he dispatched Iris, on her wings the colour of gold,
to give Demeter his orders, and she did as he asked,
covering the distance in no time, and landing
at Eleusis, where the air was filled with incense.
She found Demeter wearing dark robes in the temple,
and spoke to her urgently: 'Zeus, our father
who knows everything, summons you back now
to join the family of the immortal gods:
come quick, don't let his command be in vain.'
But her pleas had no effect at all on Demeter:
then Zeus sent out all of the gods, one by one,
to deliver his summons, bringing the best of gifts,
with whatever fresh honours she might desire;
but Demeter was so furious then that she
dismissed every speech out of hand, and told them all

that she would neither set foot again
on Olympus, nor let anything grow on the earth,
unless she could see her beautiful daughter once more.

When he heard this, Zeus, the deep- and wide-bellowing God,
sent Hermes with his golden staff down into the dark
to talk to Hades there, and ask his permission
to lead Persephone back up from the shadows
and into daylight again, where her mother
could set eyes on her, and so be angry no longer.
Hermes agreed to do this: he hurried away
from his place on Olympus, down into the earth's
crevasses and crannies, down, till he reached
the king of all the dead in his underground palace,
stretched out at his ease, and by his arm a trembling
bride, who pined still for the mother she had lost.
Coming up close to him, the god Hermes began:
'Hades, dark-haired lord and master of the dead,
my father Zeus orders me now to take away
from Erebus the royal Persephone, back
to the world, so that Demeter, when she sees
with her own eyes her daughter returning
may relent, and give up her implacable grudge
against the gods – for what she now intends
is terrible, to wipe from the face of the earth
the whole defenceless species of mortal men
by keeping crops under the ground, and then starving
heaven of its offerings. In her rage, Demeter
will have nothing to do with the gods, and she sits
closed in her own temple, apart, holding sway
there over the rocky citadel of Eleusis.'

Hades listened, with just the hint of a smile
on his face, but did not disobey the express
order of Zeus the king, and he spoke at once:
'Go, Persephone, go back now to your mother,
go in good spirits, and full of happiness,
but don't feel too much anger or resentment.
You know, I won't be the worst of all the gods
to have for a husband, brother to your father Zeus;

and here you could be the mistress of everything
that lives and moves, have the finest of honours
among the gods, while for all those failing to pay
their dues by keeping you happy with sacrifice,
proper respect and generous gifts, there will be
nothing in store but punishment for ever.'

Persephone jumped straight up, full of excitement,
when she heard what he said; but Hades, looking
around him, and then back over his shoulder,
gave her the tiny, sweet seed of a pomegranate
for something to eat, so that she would not stay
up there forever with the goddess Demeter.
Then Hades got ready his gold-covered chariot,
hitching up his own horses, and in stepped
Persephone, with the strong god Hermes beside her,
who took the reins and the whip in his hands
as both of the horses shot forward obediently
out and away, making good speed on their journey,
untroubled by the sea, or by flowing rivers,
or grassy glens, or freezing mountain tops:
they sliced thin air beneath them as they flew.

When they came to a stop, it was in front of the temple
where Demeter kept vigil; and, at the sight of them,
she ran forward wildly like someone possessed.
At the sight of her mother, Persephone leapt out
and into her arms, and hugged her, and she wept,
and the two of them, speechless, clung hard
to each other, until suddenly Demeter
sensed something wrong, and broke the embrace.
'My darling,' she said, 'I hope that down there
you didn't eat anything when he took you away?
Tell me, and tell me now: for, if you didn't,
you can stay with me for ever, and with the gods,
and Zeus, your father; but, if you did eat
anything at all, then you'll have to go back
underground for the third part of every year,
spending the rest of the time at my side: when
flowers come up in spring, and bloom in the summer,

you will rise too from the deep mists and darkness –
to the amazement of men, as well as the gods.
But how did Hades abduct you? What tricks
did he use to bring you away to the dark?'
'Mother,' Persephone answered, 'I will tell you it all.
When Hermes came for me on the orders of Zeus,
to take me out of Erebus, so you could see me
and abandon your vendetta against the gods,
I jumped for joy; but then Hades, unnoticed,
gave me the seed of a pomegranate to eat,
and made me taste it: it was sweet like honey.
I'll explain, just as you ask me to, how he
snatched me away in the first place, when Zeus
planned everything to bring me down under the earth.
We were playing together in an uncut meadow
– me and all my friends – and gathering for fun
handfuls of the wild flowers that were growing there:
saffron and irises, hyacinths, and young roses,
lilies gorgeous to look at, and a narcissus
that bloomed, just like a crocus, in the soil.
While I was taken up with that, from nowhere
the ground beneath me split apart, and out
came the great king of millions of the dead
who dragged me, as I screamed, into his gold-
covered chariot, and took me down into the earth.
Now you've heard what it hurts me to remember.'

That whole day long, they were completely at one:
each warmed the other's heart, and eased it of sorrow,
the two of them brimming over with happiness
as they hugged one another for joy again and again.
The goddess Hecate came to them and joined them;
still wearing her veil of white linen, she caught
Demeter's little daughter over and over
in her arms, and became her companion for ever.

Only then did Zeus, the deep- and wide-bellowing God,
send down to speak to Demeter her own mother,
Rhea, to reconcile her with her family.
On his behalf, she could offer whatever new honours

were needed, and guarantee that Persephone
would stay down in the darkness for only a season,
the third of a year, and the rest with her mother
and all of the gods. Rhea hurried to the task,
reaching the fields near Eleusis at Rarion
where harvests once were abundant, but now
no harvest could come up from the cropless plain
where Demeter had hidden away the white barley,
though afterwards, as the spring went on, it would
thicken and move with long corn, and the furrows
would be filled in due course with cut stalks
while all the rest was gathered up into sheaves.

Here the goddess first came down from the trackless air
and she and Demeter greeted one another with joy.
Rhea delivered her message from Zeus, and the promises
he made for Demeter, and for Persephone,
urging her daughter, 'Now, child, you must
do the right thing, and not venture too far
by keeping up this grudge of yours against Zeus:
let food grow again for people on the earth.'
Demeter could say nothing against this: she allowed
crops then and there to come from the fertile ground;
she freighted the wide world with flowers and leaves.

She went then to the men in power – Diocles,
Triptolemus, Eumolpus, and Celeus himself,
the people's leader, to give them instruction
in her liturgy and rites: all of the mysteries
neither to be questioned, nor departed from,
and not to be spoken about for fear of the gods,
a fear so great as to stop every mouth.
Whoever has witnessed these is blessed among men:
whoever has not been inducted, whoever
has taken no part in them, can expect no good
fortune when death fetches him to the darkness.

Once she had revealed all of this, Demeter
returned to Olympus and the company of the gods;
there she and Persephone, holy and powerful,

live beside Zeus himself, where he plays with thunder.
Anyone whom they favour is deeply blessed,
for they send the god Wealth to his own hearth
dispensing affluence to mortal men.

You who protect the people of fragrant Eleusis,
rocky Antron, and Paros surrounded by the sea,
Lady Demeter, mistress, bountiful goddess,
both you and your lovely child Persephone,
favour me for this hymn, give me a living,
and I will heed you in my songs, now and always.

The Wait

They would bury ashes or bodies in the evening,
then say whatever was right to say, looking
out into a bruised and sun-inflamed west
to think of the dead, and take leave of them.
There would be noise from here and there – people,
animals, carts, invisible cicadas –
and the one road to town would darken. When
everyone had gone back, and night came,
the spirit would loiter unseen by its grave,
alone and afraid to go far, anxious
for dawn, and departure then from the earth.

Sappho fr. 58

Children, take your fill of the good things
on offer from every well-dressed Muse,
and each clear note of the singing line:

my own flesh is showing its age; the head
of hair that was dark is dark no more,
and my heart makes heavy work of beating;

knees can barely carry me that once
would keep me dancing like the young deer
quickly, where now I have to draw breath.

Nothing to be done: for there's nobody
who goes on living without getting older –
just as, they say, Tithonus found out

when, crazy about him, the goddess
of dawn, with her rose-pale arms,
took him off to the edge of the earth

still fresh-faced and good-looking, only
for age to claim him in due course, while
his lover neither grew old nor died.

III

Country

1

I am making believe I
remember this drive-through town,

and the way they see you through
the glass, the way they clock you

(me: I might be related
to half of them) – big boys

recently men, ten or fifteen
years from an early death

who walk between doorways, and seem
to be chewing on their fists

(where the cellphones must be),
not for a single moment

missing me, now I'm back
(Merle Haggard) *I'm right back where*

I've really always been, with flags still
lynched at half-mast from every

other lamppost; driving out of town
in a hire car, with the music on.

2

The hotels were always like this:
light-industrial, bare

and ugly in farmers' fields.
Every weekend, the carvery

(three or four roast meats
rinsed with all-purpose gravy),

men standing at the long bar,
silent; and the Friday

dinner-dances, the weddings
on Saturdays till late.

It's all you can eat,
but I can't eat it,

and instead slow-stare
at a big satellite screen:

I know that I
should leave, but then

I just can't go;
for this is long ago

and still to come;
all different, and the same;

and the football and the races
haven't changed in thirty years.

3

On a hill far away, the masts
for radio and phone traffic, broadcasts

of all kinds, stand upright
together among drizzly clouds,

bearing up their weightless load
of signals in a relay race:

rain and the wind are overwrought
with all they carry, noon and night,

wherever, even in that place.

4

The little roads, signed off
to a townland or a farm

are the ones I turn from
by driving straight ahead,

just tilting my head
to long names of places,

although I am stone-deaf
to – say – the call

of Lungs Mission Hall,
travelling on, graceless,

and making believe
I never felt these hills'

threaded, invisible,
Jesus-wired

forcefields in even
my childhood's blood:

the pain of the Gospel,
that for the truth's sake

will separate, forsake,
part blood from blood,

all of it here still
where Gospel is heartbreak,

a high lonesome wail
for what's gone and to come,

but tired, tired.
This world is not my home.

5

Not here – an ocean away –
but somewhere very like,

the big-eyed eldest son
of 'Colonel' Monero Loudermilk

was born and raised to the hard
earth, then just walked away:

tall Ira Louvin
got drunk, learned mandolin,

got drunk, and sang
fit for heaven

love songs, gospel, *tragic songs*
of life, in high harmony

with his cherub-chopped brother;
got drunk, got Jesus,

and always got drunk again,
half rattlesnake, half man

(and that was according
to his friends), living on

to die in a wrecked car
out on some highway or other –

I didn't hear
nobody pray, dear brother –

who had cursed out his admirer,
the raw Elvis Aaron

to his face after one show
for a 'fuckin' white nigger';

who employed the telephone
cord to strangle his second

wife some, before she left him
her memento, four bullet wounds,

four bullets he carried for life;
who never was safe

to be with, safe or sound;
and who, when *the whiskey*

and blood ran together
went home to his Saviour

between hot-silvery
asphalt and the poor ground.

6

In such a state
that he won't even cross the street,

in Augher, a man my age
stands at the verge

and meets my eyes, I think,
with his tired-out eyes.

The red face is the drink:
he looks without surprise

as I leave him behind;
beyond that, a blank;

and who gives who the slip
is open as the sky,

or now the brisk two-step
(Willie Nelson) of *do you mind*

too much if I
don't understand?

7

So just how sentimental?
About 100%

and don't forget it:
power in the blood

and all the risks of that;
older, and much worse now

than when I upped and fled.
For all over town

the news is out: *soon*
his head

like mine will bow.
The tight air overhead

is jittery, alive
with music and pictures, voices

all scrambled, but not dead,
that pulse through years and places

never remote again,
and here I am *making believe*

I never lost you, a one-two-
one dance time, Patsy Cline

steel-soft, not gone,
the phrasing exact, heartbroken;

my father and my mother
still dancing to it, somewhere;

all that, and the man
on the road I left behind,

bowed, put-upon,
his head like mine.

Riddarholmskyrkan

Against the Baltic Sea
ink-lit from underneath
on that bright evening, we
watched our dispersing breath
and walked over clean stones
to where they kept their dead
kings in a stash of bones
ornate with gilded lead,
carved oak and filigree:
I thought that I could see
in there one polished wreath
made out of wood, that shone
back light from overhead
into the well-kept vault,
but I heard our living steps
that echoed to a halt
no sooner come than gone
diminish and retreat
away out through the gaps
between the sea and town
like some repeating phrase:
I could hear myself repeat
it's not my fault, or *this
isn't happening*, as though
saying would make it so.

Broken

Once I had lost you, you became
a little girl and not a woman,

a little girl who cried and cried
in the dark, as your sobs carried

across land and water; echoed
through my own cries like a chord

of grief and fear, of injustice;
made everywhere one empty space

with you lost in it, lost and scared,
knowing you couldn't be rescued:

so dawn came in with birds lamenting
daylight in their broken songs,

while the walls rang still with your cries,
accusing but defenceless,

for I could give you no comfort or shield,
and your tears were all the tears in the world.

Least

Outside, a light shuffle
where something is moving
away from or around
the house; and that sound –
the half-sound an animal
makes near home, or roving
far from it, a scratch
through twigs, grass and stones,
can leave me this once
unstartled, feeling each
noise as subliminal
work done, unplanned,
an action, for which
I simply don't matter,
not now, and not later,
all perfectly clear, and
no less than the heart's speech
abrupt, minimal.

Childhood Memories

1
The Battery Boy

As our black Ford Prefect rumbled from Stranmillis to the Braniel
on Saturday nights in winter, I looked from the back seat
at young trees in the dark, sodium lights, Belisha beacons
passing behind us through the brightened, sideways rain,
and sometimes caught sight of a solitary night-watchman
in his hut beside roadworks; I even glimpsed his face
glowing from the brazier, red cigarette and kettle
visible for a moment, thin steam from his mug of tea.

You had some name for him, a name that I repeated
with my other chant, *We're nearly home, we're nearly home,*
that lonely man who sat all night by a few coals,
watching, and breaking the dark; a name that I've forgotten,
but get back, nearly, sometimes – like today, when I
pictured a beaming face, all eyes, and called it *Torchy.*

2
1966

The first time I ever saw a man riding a horse
was when the farmer with a red face and a wig
came swaying on his saddle up the Gilnahirk Road,
beneath him the enormous white and grey creature
and coming behind him a fife band, playing *Dolly's Brae*:
I remember his drinker's nose, as well as the bright graffiti
of broken veins scribbling his cheeks, his false
curls of black hair, and the sword upright in front of him.

Aunt Ruby held my hand as we looked down from the garden
where I was frightened and agog, too small to know
that this armed man was not the actual King Billy
riding up to Mann's Corner to claim his own, or that
he would not appear after tea, huge at the parlour door,
when my uncle James recited *The Orange ABC.*

3
Souvenir d'Ypres

It was a good half-century after the battle
that my great uncle Archie, bedridden, propped-up
to talk to the boy, took one look at my model soldiers
and asked about the shiny, field-grey, moulded man
who lay flat on his stomach, with a rifle levelled
in front of him, taking aim: when I explained he was
a German sniper, Archie held him up, then laughed
and offered only, 'Aye, the snipers, they're the boys!'

I have his pocket-book, embossed A.G., inside it
an old pound note; his childhood copy of Robert Burns;
a swagger-stick, topped with silver, he had in the army,
and a brass cartridge case, the handle for a paper-knife,
marked *Souvenir d'Ypres*: that's all of him, flat out,
smiling, with his bare feet poking from the blanket.

4
Torchlight

Power-cuts in the strike added a new dimension
to the games I was playing with plastic soldiers and tanks
at the back of the sitting-room: now, in the dark,
stealthy commandos started on their midnight raid
to disable a German Panzer and a gun emplacement
under the full moon of a propped electric torch
that shone from high on the settee down to the floor,
lighting up brittle artillery and carpet pile.

Further back, the rest of the furniture was edged
with a penumbra of torchlight – the weakest shine
on a table top, the reflection of a reflection
on curving glass in the dead television screen:
shadows regrouped and shifted, as I crept to war
with the eye of a burning torch burning in my eye.

5
Blue Skies

It must be warm weather, for the front door and the hall
are both open, and I am sitting on the path
watching crowds in a field above the high Braniel
who are themselves listening to an amplified roar
that is Paisley's, unmistakably, and echoes down
this far to Woodview Drive, although his words are lost
in their own noise, and only the outrage and the scorn
come through intact on lazy, slow-dancing thermals.

I start to look instead at an almost cloudless sky,
a blue sky in fact, and I tune the new transistor
to a mixture of midsummer babble and pop music,
cushioned, buoyed up, and floating over the big noises
to *See my Baby Jive* and *Summer (The First Time)*
long after the audience has trickled from the hill.

6
Petrol

I didn't see it, although I heard about it later,
the little gift that entered straight through the front door
early one evening, when everybody was out,
and broke on the cold floor-tiles, the ox-blood tiles,
igniting in the dark for maybe a few seconds
then burning low, then fading completely away
to be found later: scattered bits of a milk-bottle,
heat-stains beneath them; the burned rag, and the smell.

I had to imagine the light it must have given out
as it spurted briefly up the flight of concrete steps
and slapped the walls and sank, then bubbled up again,
coating the red-brown floor with shapes of amber and orange
that sloped and lingered most when I would close my eyes
to press the eyelids with my fingers, all that year.

7
Bits and Pieces

One February night, my father came home shaking
with his face blank, and cold hands, not really speaking,
and although ours was a house that never kept strong drink
he needed more than water to steady him that Monday
after he'd driven from the top of the Castlereagh Road
on to the dual carriageway, where what he saw
was the bombers' car in fragments, then the four of them
scattered in lumps, being scraped up from the pavement.

A little crowd had recourse to the Dave Clark Five
as it chanted at the ambulances and fire engines
over and over the chorus from *Bits and Pieces*, while
by the garage forecourt policemen gleaned the mortal
remains of Steele and Bell, Magee and Dorrian
expertly, having done this kind of thing before.

8
The Collar

On his annual visits from Stranraer, my uncle Tom
(a great-uncle, tall and blind, unstoppable)
would put me to the test: first, it was Bible-stories,
then my catechism, and finally, when I
somehow was learning Greek, my *ho, he, to,*
known from his training days, like the boys' chorus
in the tenements of *Maw, throw us a jeely piece*
that he would bellow, laughing, decades and decades on.

He wore the collar everywhere: once, it had saved
his skin when, with his height and his bare fists,
he stopped the shipyard men lynching a Catholic;
now it got him a good seat in the Martyrs' Memorial
where he said the famous preacher spoke well, but forgot
the imperative, to hate the sin and love the sinner.

9
Kenneth

My grandmother's grave is heaped with roses and carnations
on a dark afternoon in my first flash-photograph,
and behind it, in the drizzle, Mrs Kyle is standing
with her hanky in her hand, friendless, not going home –
home where her son Kenneth might or might not be,
dapper even in his middle years, my father's best man
and like him well turned-out, a touch fastidious
although his good clothes have about them the sheen of age.

As it happens, Kenneth outlives his own mother
by only a year or two: he has fed on whisky
for so long, at the end it sweats from his every pore
and he never comes out. Mrs Kyle grips her handbag
as a flashbulb in its plastic cube erupts and blisters,
coating with light the flowers and their wet cellophane.

10
Spartans

Across the Lisburn Road, every other wall was marked
with big initials, FTP or UVF,
beneath the billboard adverts for *Harp, Old Spice: The Mark
of a Man*, or the Confidential Telephone,
and by eight on that hot evening, all the cars
had gone away, leaving a dog or two, and drinkers
quietly threading a course from lounge bar to lounge bar
while down the sidestreets footballs smacked on gable walls.

Messenia was Bradbury Place, and Thermopylae
the narrow cut outside Taughmonagh's tintown
for the Tartan gang who changed themselves from LRT
and crossed over that night as the Lisburn Road Spartans,
surrounding the hall, kicking a door in, breaking
the boy's legs like sticks, and carving his neck with LRS.

11
Saturday

We would leave the band practising noisily at school
and take the long walk down Great Victoria Street
where records might be bought, or looked over, thought about;
then a longer walk, through town, in through the barriers,
having our pockets searched, searching our pockets for change,
and striking out that day to what was left of Smithfield
to pick up some bargain Stevie had got word of:
with nothing for the bus, we trailed back the way we came.

Some RUC men gave us a lift in their armoured car
after the boys at head-level on a parapet
aimed half a dozen kicks, though none of them at me –
at Stevie, with the blood pouring from both nostrils
on his steady walk, and his head still full of music,
cradling a bag of singles as he weighed up the damage.

12
Tommy

He would see you coming half-way up Dunluce Avenue,
and specialised in a long-range, drawn-out 'Well?',
to answer which you had to approach, and go with him
at a painful crawl all the way to the Lisburn Road, where
your two paths could decently diverge; Tommy looked
much older than he was, but there was nothing of him –
unwashed and unshaven, crippled with something, his only
ports of call by then the post-office and the pub.

He stuck to the wrong names for everyone, and he crooned
impenetrable songs to himself; when he died
alone, and the tiny house was cleared then cleaned out,
for months I would still avoid him, see a filthy coat
propped up over a stick, moving, and hear him greet
my mother from a distance with 'Well, Mrs Donnelly?'

This Earth

Whenever I talk to them, they don't answer: maybe
their silence is meant to imply something – that I
should know the answers already – maybe it's just
silence, maybe they can't speak, they don't exist,
and for this job I'm going to need the god Hermes
to walk for me among the undisciplined armies
of the dead, to search out this one and that one
as they wander round without any hurry or reason
and then deliver himself of what I have to say.
He has a sad look, for all his silver skin and his finery,
having been there too often before, a survivor
of glam rock, all metallic spray-painted feathers
and glittery boots, with his make-up peeling
from an age-stricken face; now there's no telling
what music he hears while he looks at the distance
where there's no music at all, and where mischance
is the way of things. If a song can be a present,
I'll give him *Flyin' Shoes* by Townes Van Zandt
(whose ghost, when he's down there, he might well meet,
hungover and good as its word, *I don't think that
I'm going to benefit from anything on this earth*).
I'll offer him whatever all his trouble is worth,
but he's too far gone now even for country music
and mottoes like *Love is just basically heartbreak.*
He clatters away, and I know that he's not coming back.

The Cheetah

1

Cat-shaped, but bigger than a cat,
on its long string the toy balloon
rose and wandered, while you sat
tethering it this afternoon
to your right hand, correcting me
when I misread its spots, and called
the cheetah a leopard: your free
hand pointed where the creature stalled
and started on its leash; you shaped
its profile for me in the air
as you jumped to your feet, escaped
our skyless room, and there you were
outside, and I was with you, saying
not to let go, not to let go,
for fear the cheetah, toppling, swaying,
would leave us standing far below
and helpless: but you laughed and said
that was the whole idea, then
stretched one arm up over your head,
with all the cheetah's lift between
two fingers, and you opened them,
letting it jump high in the wind,
the long string trailing, helium
so light once it was unentwined
that the balloon shot upwards, flew
across the houses, over town,
but kept till it was out of view
the cat-shape of its yellow-brown.

You were delighted, and we watched
until the drifting shape was gone
entirely, and the whole sky matched
itself in patchy blue again.
I saw myself drawing a line
in the air around some dangerous
fast-moving predator of mine
that I enclosed, and filled with gas,
to set it loose into the day:
what I held, or was holding to,
could take itself up and away,
and all there was for me to do
was let it go. I almost felt
the string rise and unravel through
my fingers, like someone who knew
that he would give up everything
he had and could have, everything,
to stand here for these minutes, to
search in the empty sky with you;
and I could sense the shiny pelt
of that wild animal ascend
out of my reach for good, to live
without us at the cold, far end
of the harm we do, the hurt we give,
and join the cheetah stalking space,
not to be ours again; to be
a lost shape in some open place
high up: and that's the whole idea.

Notes

'Oxford Poetry' 2 (p. 19)

Quotations and content are taken from the Foreign Secretary Alec Douglas-Home's 'Secret & Personal' memo of 13 March 1972 to the Prime Minister, Edward Heath. (The document is to be found at the Public Records Office, as PREM 15/1004.)

'Hymn' (p. 36)

The ancient Greek *Hymn to Demeter* is one of the so-called Homeric Hymns, mythological poems (of varying lengths) which seem to have been parts of the repertoire of Homeric performers from early times. Scholars date the *Hymn to Demeter* to the sixth century BC, but unlike the other Homeric Hymns, it has been known to modern readers only since the end of the eighteenth century, when a medieval manuscript of the poem was discovered in a stable in Moscow. My translation of the *Hymn* attempts to be as faithful as possible to the Greek text. I have, however, made some cuts and compressions; I have also translated a number of epithets in ways not quite in line with what we can know about their 'literal' meaning; and occasionally I have erased particular epithets altogether. I have worked from the text of Martin L. West's *Homeric Hymns, Homeric Apocrypha, Lives of Homer* (Cambridge, Mass.: Harvard University Press, 2003), alongside the text and commentary of N.J. Richardson's *The Homeric Hymn To Demeter* (Oxford: Clarendon Press, 1974).

'Sappho fr. 58' (p. 52)

In 2004, the wrappings of an Egyptian mummy in the collection of the University of Cologne were found to contain pieces of the Greek text of Sappho (sixth century BC). One fragment in particular related to scraps of a poem discovered among the Oxyrhynchus papyri in 1922, and known since then as fr. 58: by combining the Cologne text with the existing fr. 58, scholars have produced what may well be a substantially complete lyric by Sappho. The poem appears to be in six two-line stanzas, with a few words still missing only in the first four lines. The Greek text, with a translation by Martin L. West, was published in the *Times Literary Supplement* 24 June, 2005.

'Riddarholmskyrkan' (p. 62)

The Riddarholmen Church in Stockholm, located on an island close to the Swedish Royal Palace, contains the tombs of Swedish monarchs from the early seventeenth century onwards.